T0208584

The Family Guide
to the Law of Attraction

Learn how to use the magic
of the Universe and make
stuff happen—together!

MARY PETTO

BALBOA.
PRESS
A DIVISION OF HAY HOUSE

Balboa Press books may be ordered through booksellers or by contacting:

Balboa Press
A Division of Hay House
1663 Liberty Drive
Bloomington, IN 47403
www.balboapress.com
1 (877) 407-4847

Because of the dynamic nature of the Internet, any web addresses or links contained in this book may have changed since publication and may no longer be valid. The views expressed in this work are solely those of the author and do not necessarily reflect the views of the publisher, and the publisher hereby disclaims any responsibility for them.

The author of this book does not dispense medical advice or prescribe the use of any technique as a form of treatment for physical, emotional, or medical problems without the advice of a physician, either directly or indirectly. The intent of the author is only to offer information of a general nature to help you in your quest for emotional and spiritual well-being. In the event you use any of the information in this book for yourself, which is your constitutional right, the author and the publisher assume no responsibility for your actions.

Any people depicted in stock imagery provided by Getty Images are models, and such images are being used for illustrative purposes only. Certain stock imagery © Getty Images.

Print information available on the last page.

ISBN: 978-1-9822-3602-1 (sc)
ISBN: 978-1-9822-3604-5 (hc)
ISBN: 978-1-9822-3603-8 (e)

Library of Congress Control Number: 2019915538

Balboa Press rev. date: 10/11/2019

For Paul, Tova, and Tali,
the manifestations of the intention I
set when I was 15 years old.

PREFACE

The Law of Attraction has been a part of my life since I was a kid. I manifested my first boyfriend when I was 14 on my first day at a new summer camp. The night before the first day, I made the decision to become "someone new." In my 14-year-old mind in the early 1980s, that meant the kind of person that was popular and had a lot of friends. I repeated to myself through the night, "I am popular" and "I have a boyfriend." About half-way through that first day of teen travel camp, I was hanging out with some of the other teens, telling them a story, when I became acutely aware that they were intently focused on my every word. In the distance, I saw a small group of girls, somewhat awkward, sitting together in silence. I knew in that moment that I had made a magical move: a move from quiet wallflower with a small group of friends to popular girl with a large co-ed group of friends. Then, later in the afternoon, Alex, the token "funny guy" at camp, took my hand in his and asked me if I would go out with him.

I didn't know what I did, but this new knowledge that I had some sort of magical power to get whatever I wanted set the course for all my decisions well into my early thirties. I got whatever I wanted and I found myself lacking patience for people who complained that they didn't have what they wanted. I didn't understand why they couldn't do what came so naturally to me.

However, after I got married and had two small children, I suffered for several years from anxiety. Episodes were acute; there were times that my husband would come home from work and find me curled in a ball in the corner of the kitchen. I was stricken with fear on a daily basis. Fear of death (mine and my husband's), fear for my kids' safety, fear of strangers, fear of flying, fear of food poisoning... and even social fears. I was quite a mess!

My professional job at the time, social media consultant, led me to the discovery of the book *The Secret*. It was an eye-opener, for sure. Not only did this popular book about the Law of Attraction explain what this natural law of the universe was, it was also one GIANT smack on my head! Duh, I used to understand the way the universe worked, and somewhere along the way I had forgotten.

Once I got back on track with my power, I never had another anxiety attack again. I dedicated several years to studying everything I could about how we harness this incredible power we each have, then spent many more years telling everyone about it that would listen. Eventually, my Law of Attraction coaching and speaking business evolved to the forefront, but there was one thing that continued to nag at me.

I realized that, even when my clients learned how to harness the Law of Attraction to manifest just what they wanted, somehow many returned to feeling like victims of their situations again. Sure, I'd get repeat business, but these beautiful souls who at one time had become super manifestors ended up once again trapped in relationships they didn't want, contending with bad situations in middle school, suffering from recurring health issues... one minute they "got it," and the next it was gone.

That's what had happened to me. By forgetting just how powerful I was, I lost several good years of my life dealing with fear and anxiety.

How had I forgotten?

Then it hit me. The difference between a person who consistently carries the power to manifest anything for years and a person who forgets that they have that power is whether they are surrounded by others who also know the secret. Once I figured this out, I began to coach in groups. Whether getting clusters of friends or families to self-organize for Law of Attraction and vision board workshops, or moving one-on-one coaching to include other family members in the conversations, these groups have been able to sustain their spiritual memories of their connection to the universe and the magic they can create.

It's not surprising, though, right? We are always more successful when supported by our tribe. When we are on the same page as our parents and kids, or our friends and coworkers, such as with dieting, quitting smoking, learning to change behavior issues, or sticking to a new health regimen, the results are amazing. That's because we are not alone.

This is how this book was born.

CONTENTS

INTRODUCTION

Abracadabra!

"It will be created in my words."

Is there something you want? A situation you want to change? A relationship you want to create? Something fun you want to have?

All you have to do to make your magic happen is this:

Ask. Believe. Receive.

It's as easy and as true as the magical incantation *abracadabra,* which is Aramaic for "It will be created in my words." That's how you use the Law of Attraction to make your magic happen. Sounds crazy? Maybe. But it works.

Just ask Trina.

Trina, a 9-year-old girl in fourth grade, was having a terrible time at school. Her two best friends, Jenny and Leila, had stopped including her in their hangouts and they had convinced the other girls in the class to not be friends with Trina and to not sit with her at lunch. Trina spent her days at school sitting alone, and she was sad each night as she went to bed thinking about how she had nothing to look forward to the next day at school.

But one day, Trina learned about the Law of Attraction and how to *ask, believe,* and *receive.* The very next day her entire dynamic at school changed. Those two bullies essentially vanished from Trina's life, the other girls in class sat with her and remained her friends for the rest of the school year, and even more good things followed for Trina all the way through high school.

The day Trina learned how to use her power set the course for her for years to come. You will discover the full story about how Trina used the Law of Attraction to make her bullies go away later in this book, but this is just an example of the kind of power that you, too, have within you.

CHAPTER 1

How to Use This Book

You are going to learn how to make things happen with your power to manifest what you want. With this book as your guide and your family or your friends to support you, you will be able to make big things happen as well as little things that will tickle you with delight!

*** *FAMILY TIME: Look for opportunities throughout the book that show you how to make the most of your experience as a group.*

First: Make a bookmark.

Since this is a book, and you may be sharing it, bookmarks are a pretty fundamental tool for everyone using and sharing this book.

But your bookmark will also be a magic wand!

Materials:

- Paper or cardboard or anything you can put words on.
- Pens, crayons, markers, or anything you can write words with.

Directions:

1. On one side of your bookmark, make a list of 10 things you're thankful for.
2. On the other side of the bookmark, put 10 more things that you're thankful for.

Ta-da!

Guess what! You've already started to become more powerful. That's the truth. It seems too easy, but focusing on what you are grateful for, being thankful for the things that are already making you happy, turns on the powerful vibrational energy you use to create magic!

Read the gratitude list on your bookmark each time you open the book.

Then: Read and play along together.

This book is for everyone in your home or club. If you're reading the book at the same pace, it's fun to do the experiments and projects together, too.

Always: Enjoy time together talking about how magical and powerful you are.

A key ingredient to using your Law of Attraction magic is to set daily or weekly time together. Talk about what you've learned, the fun things you've been able to manifest, what happened in the past week that you are grateful for, and what you are looking forward to in the next week. Keep the conversation going!

To supplement the high-vibe energy, think about these things as you fall asleep each night.

Finally: Make a vision board.

Now that you know how much power you have to create and have whatever you want, it's time to make a vision board—a super-cool tool to remind you what is important to you and what you want to manifest. Thousands of people have made their dreams come true by creating vision boards!

In the end:

Throughout this book there are countless stories of how people just like you tapped into their power to create new realities right before their eyes. Be sure to read Chapter 8 to discover more stories of kids and adults who used their power—the power of the Law of Attraction—to get what they wanted.

Add your own chapter:

Record all of the fun synchronicities, coincidences, and things you manifest. Write them down and tuck your notes into the back of the book so that if you ever forget how powerful you are, you can pull them out and remember!

*** *FAMILY TIME: Make your bookmarks together as a family. Share your gratitude lists with each other!*

Magic Vocabulary

There are special words you use when talking about how powerful you are with the Law of Attraction. Some of these may be everyday words for you already, but take a moment to read through them so you can understand what they mean in this book.

Universe, with a capital U – The Universe, the Source, God, or getting into the Vortex. These are all different terms that come to mean the same thing. Whether you are religious, spiritual, or a person who loves to see everything scientifically proven, you'll notice similar patterns in the practice of your power and that all roads lead to the same place. Today's quantum physics and neuroscience are beginning to prove that our spiritual or religious practices work, and the Law of Attraction is what connects you to the magic. That's when the power gets unleashed. The Universe, Source, God, or the Vortex. Whatever you want to call it, it's listening to you and wants to work for you. Together you're going to make it all happen.

Energy – Everything is made of energy, all matter comes from energy, and you use your energy every minute of the day through thoughts and actions. Where you focus your energy, then, determines the results of what you manifest.

Vibration – All energy has a vibration. Where you set your vibration will determine how the Universe responds to you.

High vibe – When the energy you put out has a high frequency. This is achieved when you feel joy, contentment, enthusiasm, gratitude, and love for your powerful connection to the Universe.

Love – Joy and gratitude. It can mean romantic love or love for one's family, but it can also mean love for your experiences and your life. It's love for all other people and for all that you have. When you do things with love you do them knowing that you have the power to live the life you want and make others feel good.

Low vibe – When the energy you put out has a low frequency. This occurs when you feel ungrateful or you feel like you have no control, or you are judging yourself or others, or make decisions based on fear. You cannot manifest what you want in a low-vibe state; you will only manifest more of what is making you feel negative.

Fear – Fear can mean feeling scared. But it doesn't just mean being scared of doing scary or uncomfortable things. Fear, when it comes to using your magic, means that you do things from a place of worry or concern. When you don't act in the way that you want because you are afraid of consequences, or you are afraid of what others think, you are in a state of fear. This is an emotion you want to avoid because it lowers your vibration and will get in the way of your power.

Manifest – To create something with your power is to manifest what you want.

Gratitude – The state of gratitude is when you are thankful, you appreciate what you have and where you are, and when you are content with the way things are right now.

Ask – To ask is to clearly decide what you want to manifest.

Believe – To believe is to know in your heart that what you want will manifest, because you are powerfully connected to the Universe.

Receive – To receive what you asked the Universe for is to keep doing things that make you feel joy and letting things unfold naturally without worry.

Visualize – Visualizing is imagining that what you want to manifest has already happened or that you already have it. Visualizing is most powerful when you also imagine what it feels like to get what you want and kindle all the energy and happy emotion around it.

Affirmations – Statements said out loud or in your head that mean that you already have what you want.

Alignment – Alignment occurs when your beliefs and actions match what you want to manifest. When you get in alignment with what you want, you are putting out the right frequency to attract all the things you want to manifest.

CHAPTER 2

Let's Get Started!

You are powerful. You're like a wizard.

Yep, whether you're 9 or 99, shy or outspoken—a doctor, teacher, student, or the town mayor—if you have dreams and things you want, you can receive them, thanks to a natural law of the universe called the Law of Attraction.

The Law of Attraction states that we attract whatever we are focused on. Because *everything* is made of energy in a range of vibrational frequencies, we attract whatever matches the range we are giving off. Our thoughts become things, and our inner language and beliefs dictate what we see. As easily as just knowing and believing that the energies of the Universe are supporting us, we can bring into our life anything we want.

I'm sure you have questions, so allow me to answer them.

How?

By working with the Universe's vibrational energy, you are always attracting everything you think about or believe.

But how?

When you decide what you want and know in your heart you can have it, the Universe will bring it to you. We're going to break down the process in this book.

Is this hard to do?

No.

Well, to be honest, it's not hard for *kids*, but for adults it can be challenging sometimes.

Does it work for everything I want?

Yes, if you are seeking things that a human would want. If what you want is to be able to grow fins and breathe under water, it might not work. It's also important to not use the Law of Attraction to manifest anything that would hurt someone.

Does it take a long time for my power to work for me?

You are always using your power; it's already working, but this book will show you how to tune in to the frequency of the new outcomes you want. Some dreams that seem impossible come true overnight. Being open to the possibilities of how your dreams will manifest will help the Universe deliver faster!

Wait, can you give me more details on this?

Sure! Everything that comes into your life you are attracting. It's attracted to you by the images you are holding in your mind. It's what you're thinking.

Your thoughts and intentions have an energetic frequency to them. You know how when you are having bad thoughts or sad thoughts you have low energy and it's hard to notice what's going on around you, but when you are happy and everything feels right, you have an extra kick in your step and things seem just a little brighter and more exciting? Your thoughts are a real thing!

Because you think and imagine and visualize, you are the most powerful magnet in the world.

It is the Law of Attraction that determines the complete order of everything. It doesn't matter who you are or where you are; everything around us is shifting to create the manifestation of what everyone is focused on.

Your life right now is a reflection of your past thoughts, and that includes all the good things and all the not-so-good things.

A primary reason there are people who don't have what they want is that they are thinking more about what they don't want than what they do want. So, if you are a complainer, the Law of Attraction brings into your life more situations for you to complain about. On the other hand, people who we think of as "lucky," people who seem to have everything go their way all the time, manifest those good things because they only expect good things to happen.

Words + Thoughts = Energy

For the Doubters

"If you change the way you look at things, the things you look at change." – Dr. Wayne Dyer

This quote—made famous by Dr. Wayne Dyer, one of the most prolific thinkers and writers on the Law of Attraction—means that our perception of the world is what creates our life experience. In other words, how we look at our life and the world around us is modified by our previous experiences.

Max Planck, known as the founder of quantum physics, was a German physicist who demonstrated that when an individual looks at an object, the characteristics of the object actually change at a very real and physical molecular level. In the next few pages, I will explain more about how modern quantum physics proves the validity of the centuries-old universal Law of Attraction.

Our memories, and the things we have chosen to believe (or deny), create our current perception. No doubt you have agreed and disagreed strongly with others when looking at exactly the same thing. For example, most people are scared by spiders, but I'm sure you know someone that is not fazed by any bug. This all depends on your previous experience and what you have established in your mind as acceptable or not.

Think of something that you used to be afraid of or disliked but eventually overcame (fear of the dark or public speaking, distaste for coffee or vegetables). As soon as your perception was flipped, that thing became something different—it went from bad to good, from yuck to yum. This is the flip I am expecting you to take while reading this book. When you do, you will join thousands of new creators that are reaping the benefits of the Law of Attraction, and you will be supported by concepts both firmly established and newly validated.

Let's look at how science has brought us to this point over time.

You may have heard of scientists like Galileo and Copernicus. Talk about changing perspectives! Galileo was the first to theorize that the earth and other planets revolved around the sun. This went against the firm beliefs of the day, but today it is scientifically proven and universally accepted.

Later, Isaac Newton published his theories on gravity, and his laws of motion created the basis for understanding that the universe appears to work in a precise and mathematical manner, like clockwork.

Discovering Consciousness

During the era of Galileo, there wasn't a lot of focus on concepts like soul, spirit, or consciousness. But just before Newton was born, Rene Descartes, the French "father of philosophy," declared that the best way to understand how the world works would be to divide existence into two parts: the objective, material world governed by the principles of science, and the subjective world of the mind and the soul, which would be understood by religion. Descartes' famous statement,

"I think, therefore I am,"

brought the worlds of the objective and the subjective together. He bridged the gap by wrapping his head around these concepts: How is it that we think? Where do our thoughts come from? How do the bits of physical matter and energy that constitute our brains generate awareness or consciousness?

In the late 1890s, concurrent with the discovery of radioactivity, scientists began to look within the atomic nucleus, where they discovered that on the subatomic level, the physical world did not behave the way physicist Isaac Newton said it should. The atom itself, it seemed, was actually like an illusion: the closer scientists looked, the less it appeared to be there.

In the beginning of the 20th century, Albert Einstein, a mathematician, found that the only way to explain the behavior of light was to stop looking within the framework of traditional Newtonian physics. Instead, he introduced a new picture—the theory of relativity.

Energy and Vibrations

The theory of relativity was groundbreaking because it described how energy and matter are not only related but can be transformed back and forth into each other. This concept was the beginning of quantum physics—the study of how the world works on a level far smaller than the atom.

Einstein's breakthrough comes down to this:

Everything is energy. Everything you can taste, touch, or smell is made of molecules. What you're made of, atoms, is literally vibrating packets of energy.

Twenty years after Einstein's work, scientists Niels Bohr and Warner Heisenberg realized that when you take a deeper look at atoms, they aren't just protons, neutrons, and electrons. At the even smaller level, atoms are really made up of tiny packets of energy called *quanta* that have the potential to become anything. The work of Bohr and Heisenberg suggested that physical matter – reality and real things – are not made of solid substances, but of fields of energy, and that a particle takes on the specific character of a material thing only when it is measured or observed.

Thought is where everything comes from.

The truth is we don't see what is there; we see what we are prepared to see and what we are conditioned to see. Your beliefs don't simply reflect your reality— they *create* your reality. *The idea precedes the thing.* Or, stated another way,

You've got to *believe* it to *see* it!

Dr. Fred Alan Wolf, an authority on quantum physics and consciousness, says quantum physics dictates that you can't have a universe without the mind entering into it. The mind is actually shaping what we perceive. In *Taking the Quantum Leap: The New Physics for Nonscientists,* Dr. Wolf writes, "The gradual recognition that what we think may physically influence what we observe has led to a revolution in thought and philosophy, not to mention physics." In *The Dreaming Universe: A Mind-Expanding Journey into the Realm Where Psyche and Physics Meet*, Wolf explained, "In order for a reality to be created, a quantum wave had to travel out to the future, and a feedback from the hoped-for future event had to return in time to the present. This mixture of waves was responsible for the way things are now."

So there it is—the discovery that the act of observation influences the behavior of atomic particles. The action of consciousness upon a piece of matter, then, is what creates our reality.

This is where quantum physics intersects with thoughts, intention, and visualization. What quantum physicists have found has everything to do with the Law of Attraction and how you're going to create the outcomes that you want. Thanks to quantum physics, we now know that everything is energy and that there is no absolute distinction between matter and energy. The boundaries between the physical world and the world of our thoughts are blurred.

Here's all you need to know:

- **Everything in the physical world is made of atoms.**
- **Atoms are made of energy.**
- **Energy is influenced by consciousness.**

Imagine what can happen if we believe that only the best of everything is happening to us and around us!

Abracadabra – Magical Weight Loss

A pair of researchers named Alia Crum and Ellen Langer wanted to test what the impact was of changing beliefs and perceptions about everyday activities. In their experiment, they were focused on creating weight loss. They used the housekeeping staff at several different hotels for the testing grounds.

First, they met with the crews at each hotel to determine their current beliefs around their jobs and exercise. While the crews were in fact very active throughout their shifts, the researchers determined that the staff did not believe that they got much exercise throughout the day. Not surprisingly, their weights and measurements were in alignment with their beliefs.

Next, the researchers told the crews of some of the hotels that their daily activities really are good exercise and shared with them how many calories were burned for each task they did. The other crews received no information.

Guess what happened! One month later, the housekeepers who were told that their work was good exercise lost weight and inches and had indications that other facets of their health were improved, even though their work did not change. And, it should not surprise you to learn that the group that was not informed of the good news about their daily activity showed no change in their weight or health as they continued to believe that their work didn't count as important physical activity.

Abracadabra – Creating Successful Students

In the previous experiment, it was illustrated that by changing our beliefs we can have a direct impact on our own health with vibrational intention. But your expectations of *other people* have such a strong vibration that it can even affect student success in the classroom. A Harvard professor named Robert Rosenthal did an experiment in 1964 to prove this is the case.

In Rosenthal's experiment, he provided teachers with false student IQ scores and explained that the high IQ results that some of the students received were predictors of their impressive academic potential. After two years of providing this fake information to the teachers, Rosenthal discovered that those teachers' expectations of the children had a direct effect on them; those students actually achieved higher IQ scores at the end of the two-year period compared to others who were not called to the teachers' attention with phony IQ scores.

If a teacher's expectations of a student's potential

can affect their learning success, imagine what can happen in your difficult relationships when you change your vibrational frequency by shifting your expectations of the other person!

***FAMILY TIME: There's a bonus experiment toward the end of his book, Chapter 9, that will illustrate that how you engage vibrationally with others can have a direct effect on their ability to thrive. You can start this experiment at any time.

CHAPTER 3

Prove It

Did you know that human beings are made up of the same elements as the stars? We are literally made of stardust!

But the fact that the universe is actually part of us and that we are one with it isn't the only cool scientific proof that we are magical.

As explained in the last chapter, scientists like Albert Einstein have discovered that everything is made up of energy. You may have learned that we are made of molecules, atoms, protons, neutrons, and electrons. Now you know that there is an even smaller component to those components. Deep down inside an atom, below the level of protons, neutrons, and electrons, are energy packets called quanta. Depending on how fast those quanta are moving, which is their vibration, different things may form. Everything around you, even the chair you are sitting on and your best friend, are actually made of energy slowed down or sped up.

But here's the most important discovery of all:

Because everything is made up of energy, and energy moves at certain vibrational frequencies, we can attract things to us by matching their same vibrational energy frequency with our thoughts and emotions.

Coincidences

Did you ever think about a friend you haven't seen or talked to in a long time, or someone from your class or work, curiously wondering what they are up to, and then the next day they are right in front of you on line at the store? This is an example of being on an energetic frequency pattern and attracting that matching result.

What you think about you bring about.

HOT TIP: Don't think about or focus on people you don't like, because whether or not your thoughts bring you joy, the Law of Attraction is always at work and you will definitely find yourself face-to-face with that annoying person you don't like, and that won't be fun!

Parking Spot People

Here's another example of tapping into an energetic frequency. There are people who claim that they always get a good parking spot right in front of wherever they are going. Maybe you are one of these people. You say it all the time: "I always get good parking spots." And then, lo and behold, you do! How did you engage your magic?

People who proclaim they always get good parking spots not only know it's true based on past experience, they *believe* that this will always be true, and they don't doubt it for a moment. It is this "knowing thought" that sends out a frequency that, according to the Law of Attraction, must be matched in return. They are putting out a message to the Universe with their thoughts and emotions that they are a great manifestor of parking spots, so that's exactly the result that they receive.

Experiments

Let's test out this pattern and see if the Universe is listening to you. Try one or both of these experiments.

Experiment 1: Ask for a sign.

You may have heard of people asking for signs from the Universe. Usually the person is asking for spiritual support that it's okay to move forward with something or to validate that a good decision was made. In this experiment you are going to ask for a sign, but you get to pick what that sign is, and it's just so that you and the Universe can illustrate your connection to each other. It's easy and will provide you with proof of your connection to the Universe and your ability to conjure up bigger things.

All you need to do is decide very clearly in your mind what the sign is that you want to see so that the Universe can prove that it is matching your request. Think of something that's not too typical to see so that you know it really is the sign you were looking for. Don't choose things like a traffic light, a squirrel, or a blue sneaker, unless those things are very rare where you live.

I love doing this experiment because sometimes I get results right away, and other times not until the last second, and in the craziest ways! So here are the steps:

1. Pick your sign. My favorite sign is a clown because clowns are weird and a little creepy.
2. Say out loud "Universe, prove that you're listening to me and that I can attract whatever I think about. Within the next 24 hours, show me a _____.

3. Set a timer for 24 hours.

Abracadabra—Make me a lake!

One time I did this experiment in the morning while I was brushing my teeth. I said out loud "Okay Universe, show me a sign that you're listening by delivering a lake!" I chose a lake because I had just been reading a travel magazine and there was a picture of a lake on the cover. I then went into my office, turned on my computer, and walked away from it to make coffee while it booted up. When I returned to the computer, I almost dropped my coffee. There was a new wallpaper image on the home screen; my computer had decided to show me a beautiful lake at sunset between two mountains.

Abracadabra—Show me a clown!

Another time I asked the Universe to show me a clown. As I mentioned, I find clowns creepy (apologies to the clowns out there). It was right after I had dinner with my family. We had been talking about how the Universe is always supporting us. When dinner was over, I requested that the Universe show me a clown, I made a note of the time, and then forgot about it. The next night we were out for dinner in a restaurant that served Chinese food. On our placemats were pictures of the symbolic animals of the Chinese zodiac. This reminded me about the sign I had been looking for, and I noticed that there were only 30 minutes left for the Universe to show me a clown. I also noted that there was no way we were going to be out of this Chinese restaurant within the next half hour.

I had a small moment of doubt that I would see my clown sign. But I quickly restored to believing and trusting my connection to the Universe. Just then, my husband said to one of my kids "you should reach out to that girl in your class and ask her how she's doing." This triggered a memory of a TV commercial jingle from my childhood that went "reach out, reach out and touch someone." I sang it out loud, and my husband joined in. The funny thing was, we didn't know what the commercial was for. So, I did what anyone would do—I Googled the jingle. The search resulted in: *Bell Telephone commercial* and a screenshot of the commercial itself. In the screenshot was a phone booth, and inside that phone booth was *the scariest clown I had ever seen.*

Just in time but never late, the Universe had given me a wink ;)

Experiment 2: Ask for a gift.

I thought the first experiment was my favorite but this one that I first learned about from author Pam Grout is really my favorite! This one is so much fun and very rewarding!

Here is the only step:

In your mind or out loud, very clearly ask the Universe to deliver you a special gift by saying something like "Universe, I'm really looking forward to receiving an unexpected gift in the next 48 hours. Thank you!"

I've suggested this experiment to many of my clients and the results have been wonderful. Letters in the mail from long-lost friends, getting gift cards in the mail, getting asked out by a coworker, getting a raise... the list of unexpected gifts goes on! Once when I did this experiment, I was traveling on a business trip, and while I was in transit I asked for the unexpected gift. Two nights later I was in my hotel room and received a text message from my husband that a check arrived in the mail. It was for $89 from a doctor's office reimbursing me for overpayment from an appointment I had six months earlier. We went on a nice romantic date as soon as I got home from the trip using that surprise $89.

Abracadabra—Show me I'm on the right path!

A therapist colleague of mine, Molly, did the same experiment and got a different kind of unexpected gift.

She made her request of the Universe and the next day was sitting in a subway train overcome with the feeling that she wasn't good enough to be a therapist. She actually started to get weepy. She thought to herself, *I don't know if I'm really good at helping people.* At that very moment an older woman got on the train and collapsed into her seat. She was moaning and swaying back and forth and was clearly scared. Without hesitation, Molly jumped up and ran to her and, while it was hard to understand the woman because she was breathing so fast, she was able to determine that the woman had a fear of the train. Molly worked with her to get her to calm down and enlisted the help of another passenger to determine where she should get off the train next. Once the woman was taken care of, Molly found herself very grateful for that moment. Just when she thought that she had no value professionally, the Universe delivered an unexpected and powerful moment to illustrate how good she is at helping people in distress.

*** FAMILY TIME: Do these experiments together! Talk about which one you're each going to try. For Experiment 1, you don't have to share what sign you are asking for, but it will be fun to report back to each other about what happened!*

CHAPTER 4

Manifesting Step One: ASK

You can ask the Universe for anything, and you can ask at any time. When we get into step two, which is *believe*, you'll learn how to make that "ask" its most powerful, but first you need to do this: Decide what you want.

To decide is to ask.

To decide is to be very clear about the outcome you want.

When you are deciding what you want, be sure to follow these rules:

Rule 1: Don't be judgmental or feel bad about asking.

The Universe is like a big catalog. Everything you want is already available, whether it's a job, good grades, a relationship, or a new car. So go ahead, ask for what you want. There's no reason to feel guilty. Whatever it is, you deserve it! The Universe wants you to be happy, and if what you want brings you joy, then that's that!

Rule 2: Think big.

The Universe works in mysterious ways, and recognizing that it is mysterious and magical is one of the secret clues to manifesting. Therefore, it's important to focus on the end result and not break down what you want into the steps you think need to happen to get the results you want. For example, if you want to go on a girls' trip to Europe with your best friends that you can't afford right now, don't ask the Universe for $5,000, just ask for the trip! Avoid thinking about all the steps involved.

Rule 3: Make sure it feels really good.

When you are thinking about what you want, whether it's something you want forever or just for the next day, be sure that it will truly bring you joy. Another way to think of it is that what you want to manifest should be so in alignment with you, that just the thought of it makes you feel amazing.

Create your list!

When you begin learning how to make the Law of Attraction work for you, it's great to start by actually making a list. Get out a piece of paper and a pen and start writing about what you want. Whether it's several things or lots of detail around one particular subject, just let your pen roll across the paper.

*** FAMILY TIME: Create your lists together. Whether you sit down for a 10-minute list-writing session or you prompt each other when one of you is seeking something new or a change, it's good to remind one another that what you want is as close as getting a clear picture of what that thing or situation is.

Here are some things that people have asked for (and received!):

- ❖ A new job close to home
- ❖ Getting accepted to a program that they had previously been rejected from
- ❖ Doubling business sales in a week
- ❖ New romantic relationships
- ❖ Getting a seat assignment changed in science class
- ❖ Enrolling a child in an expensive summer camp when there wasn't enough money for it

❖ A dream vacation in Malibu

❖ A mean teacher transforming into a nice one

❖ Invitations to important events

❖ Health recovery

❖ New friendships

❖ A house on the beach

❖ A drama-free end to a toxic friendship

❖ A massive career promotion

❖ The exact wedding dress admired in a fake photo that came in a picture frame

❖ All the best shifts at work

Abracadabra—Send my kids to camp!

When my kids were in grade school, I launched a new marketing company with great success. However, as the first summer season was just around the corner, I wondered how I would keep the momentum going. If the kids were home, I would have very limited time for my work, and the local rec camp only covered six weeks of the summer with short days that got cancelled if it rained. Just as my concern reached its height, my kids came to me to share that they wanted to go to a very cool day camp about 20 miles away. The camp had an eight-week program each summer and the days were as long as a full work day. It sounded great—except for one thing: this camp was way out of our budget, as were other camps just like it in the area. But the more I thought about this kind of summer experience, the more I wanted it for my kids as an ongoing summer lifestyle, not just for one summer.

So, I decided. Definitively and clearly—my kids were going to be fancy-summer-camp kids. Not only did I want the time for work, but I also wanted them to have memorable experiences and enjoy the fresh air for as much time as possible before school was back in session. I didn't think or worry about how I was going to pay for it. I just decided. I then moved forward with calling around to all the camps and asking questions about their programs. One conversation I had with a camp director just naturally led into a discussion of my company, and before I hung up the phone, I had bartered for full summer sessions at the camp for both of my kids in exchange for marketing services. And the best part— the contract got renewed every year for five years. I didn't know that was going to happen when I made that call that day. As a matter of fact, bartering my services had never even occurred to me. It was the camp owner I was speaking with who brought it up. Imagine that! The Universe delivered exactly what I wanted, and in a most surprising way!

I decided.

I moved forward without worrying about the money.

I manifested five summers of incredible experiences for my two kids that would have cost $45,000 over those years. I felt like I had won the lottery!

Asking in the Moment

Once you get really practiced at asking for what you want (*deciding* what you want), and you learn to feel that it's yours with confidence (which we'll get into in Step Two), you'll find that you can manifest what you want from moment to moment. Your life will feel like the waters are parting for you everywhere you go!

Abracadabra—Give me 15 extra minutes!

One of my clients, Beth, has become well-practiced at how to ask the Universe for what she wants. She is so practiced at it that manifesting what she needs throughout the day comes very easy to her. For example, one morning she had a ton of errands to do. She needed to run to a craft store, call a contractor that she had been corresponding with on social media, run to the optometrist to pick up a pair of glasses she ordered, and then meet a friend for lunch who only had an hour to spare. After all that was done, she herself needed to get back to work, as she had taken the morning off to take care of her errands.

When she made her first stop at the craft store, things started aligning for her right away: in the paint aisle she recognized the face of the contractor she was supposed to call 30 minutes later. She said hello and they had an extended conversation because they learned they had many things in common. But by the time she made her purchase and got back in her car, she realized she was 15 minutes behind and if she went to get her glasses from the optometrist, she would be late for her lunch date. So she said out loud "I need 15 extra minutes." Almost immediately, she received a text message from the friend who was meeting her for lunch and the message said "Sorry, Beth, I'm running a little bit late. Can we meet 15 minutes later? It's OK because my plans for after lunch have been canceled." So just like that, Beth manifested what she needed.

Now 15 extra minutes may not seem like much, but it was just what Beth asked for and she knew how to align herself with the result she was seeking and received it. Imagine what this will be like for you when you become naturally aligned with the source of your power and live a life in flow like this every day!

*** *FAMILY TIME: As you fall asleep at night, decide what you want to happen the next day. Whether it's doing well on a math test or rocking a presentation at work, setting your intentions for the results you want the night before will jump-start the magic!*

CHAPTER 5

Manifesting Step Two: Believe

"A belief is just a thought you continue to think."
— Abraham Hicks

Now that you know, with clarity, what you want, it's time to get your thoughts and beliefs aligned with it. When you do, by the Law of Attraction, you will attract what you asked for with your energy vibration.

Learning to really believe that you already have what you want is the most important step to manifesting any situation. By excitedly and joyfully believing that you already have an abundance of money, that you have already gotten accepted to your college of choice, or that your relationship with your sister is terrific, you are setting the vibration emanating from your new mindset, and the Universe will reveal to you all of the situations, people, ideas, and clues that align with your new beliefs.

When you did experiment number one in Chapter 3, asking for a sign, you were actually engaging this *believe* step. You did it by choosing something to focus on, and your brain locked it down as being important to you. Your vibrational tone was set for that butterfly, purple feather, or crazy clown. You didn't have to repeat the word over and over again for 24 hours. You made a decision, and that decision became your belief when you told the Universe that you wanted to see it.

What You Believed Until Today

Way too often, things don't work out for us and we don't get what we want. But we knew it all along, right? Thoughts like "that's never gonna happen," "I'll never get what I want," and "the chances of that are very slim" are also part of your belief system, so of course you're not surprised when you were right, right? You believed that it wasn't going to work out and so it didn't.

We believe that our annoying friends are going to continue to be annoying and they are. We believe that we will never be able to break out into the profession we want, that we're stuck in the school situation that we were handed...the list goes on of the things that we "know" to be true. Then, voilà, we are right!

I'm sorry to have to tell you this, but that is the Law

of Attraction at work! You believed it wouldn't work out, so it didn't.

But what if you believed it *would* work out? What if you believed that the bullies at school were going to stop targeting you? What if you believed that the difficult person at work was going to support you at your meeting today? What if you believed that an opportunity would come up for you that you hadn't even thought about? And then, what if everything good you believed would happen actually *did* happen, just like when your beliefs were negative and bad things manifested?

The Field of Potentiality

Everything you want to receive and make happen already exists in the Universe. The Universe in this sense is often referred to as a "field of potentiality." Everything that we could ever want already exists in this quantum field, but it takes an alignment with, or embodying of, what we want in order to bring it forward into our view.

There are billions of bits of information out there swirling around us all the time. The thing is, our brains only have the capacity to take in a limited amount. So everything we see is literally aligned with what our brain already thinks is important to us. When something new becomes of interest to us or becomes important to us, our neural networks, the little wires in our brain, take note of it, lock in place, and then let in all the information that aligns with that new interest. Now our thoughts are new ones that vibrationally align with what we want. Here's a common example of how this happens all the time…

Purple Cars

There's a fun phenomenon that many of us have experienced that I like to call the "purple car principle." Did you ever notice a new model or style car you've never seen before, and think, "hey, that's a cute car, and what a great color, too," then the next time you're out on the highway there are dozens of that same car? You think, "wow, where did all these purple cars come from so suddenly?" Well, they were there on the road all along, but you literally couldn't see them because it was information that your brain concluded it didn't need; your mind and thoughts were not focused on those cars being of any importance to you. That is, until one happened to catch your eye and you decided that it was cool.

How to Believe

A well-known technique many athletes use to perform well on the field or on the court is to spend time doing mental practice. This visual rehearsal of making the shot or breaking the record is very productive. Whether your body is physically moving, and your eyes are seeing it happen in real time, or it is happening in your mind, your brain doesn't know the difference and is aligning with the high score. Those regions of the brain are stimulated either way and the same neural networks are created. The results are proven and very real.

So after you decide that you are going to be the star of the team, the popular kid in class, or a senior executive at your company, the next step is to believe it and know so deep in your heart that the result is real that you feel both relaxed and excited! The best techniques to get you to that place are visualization and affirmation.

Visualize!

Once you've gotten clarity on what you want, all you have to do is imagine that you already have it! So let's say what you want is to live in Europe for three months. Hopefully you've gotten clarity around all the pieces of that—the kind of place you'd stay in, what you would do there, perhaps how you would work from there, etc. To visualize this, follow the steps:

1. Get yourself into a very relaxed state. You can do this following some deep breaths in a comfortable spot with your eyes closed. You can also consider

doing this just after you've woken up in the morning, or as you're drifting off to sleep.

2. Empty your mind of other thoughts. My favorite way to do this is to focus on the sounds around me. (If you find your mind wandering back to your homework or to-do list, just acknowledge that you went off track and go back to emptying your mind.)

3. Next, picture yourself already living in Europe. I like to start my visualizations by picturing waking up on a new day on which I have already manifested what I want. So for this vision, you would imagine all of the details of waking up in the bedroom of your European home, what the place you are staying in looks, sounds, and smells like. Imagine where you have your laptop set up and who you're with. Imagine walking through the streets of the fabulous foreign city and take in all the details of the scenes. Even look down at your own feet as you're walking. Notice what shoes you're wearing, what the people around you look like.

4. While you're doing creative visualization, it's really important to tap into the emotions that come up. Notice the joy that you feel and how content you are having manifested just what you wanted! Let your inner wisdom guide you through the process. It can be a lot of fun!

The more details and emotion you apply to your vision, the better and tighter the neural connections are becoming for this to be part of your new belief system. Embodying this new belief will help you become more aware of the things that will make this all happen for you, things that the Universe is delivering to you through the vibrational intention you are setting.

*** FAMILY TIME: You can carve out time daily or several times each week to do this together as a family. Playing relaxing yoga music can help you stay attached to your visions, and setting a timer can help as well so you don't stop short to see what time it is.

Affirmations

Affirmations are another way to create new neural connections in your mind and become a believer in the manifestation of what you want. Affirmations are a ton of fun and can be done all the time, even while you're with other people, in class, or driving to work.

So, what's an affirmation? An affirmation is simply a statement or story that reinforces your beliefs and neural pathways. We are constantly repeating affirmations, whether we are aware of it or not. Unfortunately, we tend to affirm the beliefs that no longer serve us or are the complete opposite of what we really want.

Here are some examples of affirmations that aren't good for you but are commonly repeated in people's minds:

I will never be successful.

I am overweight.

I will never find love.

I don't have any good friends.

I'm bad at math.

The problem with these subconscious affirmations is that even if you overcome familiar patterns and find a girlfriend or lose weight, you will probably gain back the pounds or somehow sabotage the good relationship because you've wired your brain with "I am overweight" and "I don't deserve to be happy."

The right affirmations, however, can shift your reality at a rapid pace. By simply repeating statements that align with what you really want, you will replace the limiting and negative thoughts and unleash your power to change things with your new intention.

Abracadabra—Fix my school day!

I once worked with a boy, Evan, who was a

sophomore in high school. He was regularly unhappy and uncomfortable at school. When we talked about what would make things better, it turned out that he felt isolated from his friends. He felt helpless because in his longest class of the day the teacher had assigned seats and put him on the opposite side of the classroom from his friends. Whenever there was a break or they had to work in groups, he missed out on the little conversations his friends were having and he was stuck working with the kids that didn't say much. And in Evan's gym class, the coaches had created a split-class environment where, again, he was separated from his friends, and to make matters worse, the kids he was assigned to be with always picked him last for team activities.

I explained to Evan how he could magically change everything if he just believed it was possible. At first, he was hesitant that this could possibly work. His teacher had warned them in September not to ask for a seat change because this arrangement was permanent, and why on earth would the coach change her setup for gym class?

But I reminded him that the Universe has no limits, and that if he got his beliefs in alignment with what he wanted it would all happen for him.

So, Evan spent a few minutes before bed that night

imagining what it would be like to sit with his friends in class and do warm-ups with other friends in gym. He also imagined how great it would feel to be picked among the first for basketball because he was with these friends.

Then he created just two simple affirmations:

I sit with my friends in biology.
I hang with my friends in gym.

Evan fell asleep that night feeling great as he imagined a new day at school with everything working out as he wished it to, while repeating his affirmations, "I sit with my friends in biology. I hang with my friends in gym."

Evan couldn't wait to call me the next afternoon. "I can't believe it," he said. "When I woke up this morning I was in a good mood, even though I had forgotten what I was doing as I fell asleep last night. Then at school my teacher came into the classroom and announced that we were moving into a new lesson and he scrambled us up for the new lab experiment—and he put me with two of my friends. At the end of class, he said that since the lab would take several days, these were our new permanent seats! Then later in the day, when I had gym, there was a substitute teacher who said she would be with us for a few months. Then she told us to split ourselves up for a game of volleyball, and of course I got to be with my friends. I just can't believe how powerful I feel!"

Create your affirmations.

Take out a piece of paper and refer back to your list of all the things you've asked the Universe for in Step One. Turn each one into a single statement that means that you *already* have what you want, or your dream has *already* come true.

Let's say you weigh 155 pounds, but you want to lose about 40. Create an affirmation that states that this has already happened. So, if your "ask" list says, "I want to lose 40 pounds," your affirmation should be "I weigh 115 pounds." See the difference? When you got clarity on what you wanted, it was something in the future, but when you create an affirmation you are stating it as if it is your present truth. You might even want to add: "I'm very comfortable in my healthy, slender body" or "I have fun shopping for clothes because I feel confident in everything I try on," and "I look great in bathing suits." As another example, if you want to manifest living in a house on the beach, you might create affirmations such as "I have a beautiful modern home on the beach" and "I hear the ocean waves each morning from my bedroom."

*** *FAMILY TIME: It's fun and helpful to sit together while you each create your own affirmation list. Help each other turn your "asks" into positive affirmation statements.*

Rules for "Believe"

Don't use don't. It's important to not use negative words in your affirmations. Words are symbols, and the Universe and vibrational energy respond to symbols. Words like "no" and "don't" and "can't" are not part of the equation as far as the Universe is concerned. So, let's say what you want is to no longer be in debt, or maybe you just don't want to have any homework for the rest of the week. You can't state "I don't have any debt," nor can you say, "I don't have any homework this week." The vibrational energy is resonating on the words "debt" and "homework." Ultimately, you'll just end up with more debt and more homework! It's better to think of your affirmations like this: "I have all the income I need and live comfortably. I can spend my money on anything I want. I have an abundance of money." As far as the homework goes, try this instead: "I can do whatever I want after school; my schedule is totally free."

Don't ask how. As soon as you start thinking about *how* your goals and dreams could possibly manifest, you are doubting your power and your connection to the Universe, and when you doubt this connection, you are shifting to a low vibration in which you can't see the clues the Universe is leaving for you. If you wonder at all about how it's going to happen, wonder with child-like excitement, not with any doubt in mind.

Relax. The most important rule about step two, *believe*, is to really believe the Universe is listening to you. If you know that the Universe has what you want and is going to give it to you at some point, you don't cry, stress, strain, or struggle trying to get that thing. If you are anxious and "working hard" to manifest what you want, you are not believing that it's coming to you by way of the Law of Attraction. The only emotions around what you're feeling should be joy, because the only thing you believe is that you've already magically manifested what you wanted.

Abracadabra—Give me a promotion!

This is my favorite story to illustrate just how important it is to relax and believe that what you want is already yours.

A friend of mine named Tori had a really good job with an international media company. One day, Tori was asked by the management team to take on a special project for which she would have to move to another country for a year. Tori was hesitant, but she was promised that after the project was complete, she could return to the main office near her home and she would receive a promotion at that time. She had never imagined herself as an Executive Director of a department, which would be the next step up for her, but she was excited at the possibility.

So, Tori set out and temporarily moved abroad to work on the special project assigned to her. She did a great job, and when it was done, she returned to her main office near her home. Back at her old job, she wondered about the promotion she was promised. After several weeks, she finally asked the management team about the promotion. She was told that there were no current opportunities and she was given some apologies. Tori was very upset and fought as politely as she could, explaining to anyone who would listen that she was promised a promotion if she uprooted herself and managed the project.

After months of struggling to find justice, Tori had a moment of realization: First, she realized there were only a limited number of Executive Director positions at the company and that someone would have to be fired from their position to make room for her, which she knew wasn't reasonable. But more importantly, Tori realized that she was Executive Director material and that she deserved the title. She could imagine herself in the role, and she decided that it didn't matter whether the title was given to her formally. She knew in her heart that that's what she was meant to be, and she surrendered to the Universe and stopped making a fuss. Two weeks later, her boss called to tell her that he was resigning from his position to work for another company and that the management team had recommended Tori to be his replacement—Executive Director for an entire department!

Tori never imagined that her beloved boss would leave the company, so it didn't occur to her that the opportunity for her promotion was just down the hall. But the Universe needed Tori to simply believe that she was already an Executive Director, sending out the right vibrations and trusting that the Universe would deliver. Struggle and negativity just don't work when it comes to manifesting what you want. Fear that you won't get what you "deserve" is never the way to ensure that the Universe hears you. Just relax and believe!

HOT TIP 1: Keep your affirmations list handy and read it frequently. It's a good idea to state these affirmations after you do some visualization. But you can say the statements all day long. You can even create new ones as situations come up in the moment.

HOT TIP 2: If you find yourself starting to not believe, or things start to feel like they're going wrong, state this affirmation that I learned from one of my favorite spiritual icons, Abraham Hicks:

"Everything always works out for me."

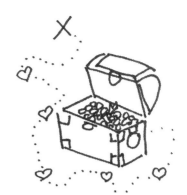

CHAPTER 6

Manifesting Step Three: Receive

You might be thinking, "Why is 'receive' a step? Do I just open my arms and wait for it?"

In a word, yes. That's the mindset you should have. You know it's coming. You don't sit with an eyebrow raised, lips pursed, arms crossed, saying "yeah, I'll believe it when I see it." You already know you must believe it *in order* to see it. Imagine that you receive a phone call that you won tickets to a concert, a shopping spree at your favorite toy store, or maybe you won the lottery! When you hang up from that phone call, you are ecstatic about your win. That money or those tickets are yours. You feel great and even start planning as if the money or tickets are already in your hands. Even though the check hasn't gotten into your hands yet, you have already won--that's the mindset and want you to be in.

Now listen to your heart and your gut.

Career opportunities and new homes don't just manifest by landing next to you in your living room. It would be cool though, wouldn't it? You visualize your brand-new bicycle, you say your affirmations regularly, and any time you get the chance you close your eyes and picture yourself riding it. When you open your eyes, though, that bike isn't parked next to you in your bedroom. But no worries. To find what the Universe has brought you, all you have to do is follow your instincts and your heart.

Go through each day doing what you want to do and going where you want to go. That's it! Without ever judging what you should do, just do it! If you feel like going to the movies, go to the movies. If you feel like reading a book on your porch even though you should call your aunt Dotty because your mother told you to, go with the book for a while. Just do what you want! Moment to moment, you need to follow your intuition and your joy. Why? Because when you do this, the Universe is putting all the clues and the components you need to manifest what you want into your view. But the only way it knows how to lead you is through your joy. And you know what else? You can't see the opportunities unless you're feeling good.

As Abraham Hicks has emphasized, the basis of your life is freedom, but the purpose of your life is joy. So if the purpose of manifesting your best life, a life in which you receive all the great things that you want, is joy, then your way to them is to stay in a place of joy. Your gut instincts are what keep you satisfied and lead you there. Remember, you are powerful, and if your gut tells you to move away from a person and toward another person, you should do that. If your gut tells you that you should take time to talk to the old friend you see at the grocery store instead of worrying about being late for an appointment, go talk to that old friend. You have the freedom to choose to move toward what feels right.

The Universe delivers its gifts to you when you allow yourself to do what you feel is best and is your guide in every decision and movement. It will show itself to you through the conversation you have with that friend in the grocery store; you might find out that her brother is selling his shore house and just wants to get rid of it quickly. Or the Universe might speak to you through a commercial about a bicycle sale that you saw on TV because you allowed yourself to take a break from homework for a little while. The Universe will keep bringing you the components you need to manifest what you want, as long as you choose to stay in a place where you feel like what you're doing is right for *you*.

Now I'm not saying you shouldn't do your homework and show up to class without it. And I'm not saying that the things on your task list shouldn't be done either. But if you wait until you feel the moment is right, you're going to tackle that homework and that to-do list like a champ! When we force ourselves to do things with this feeling that we *should* do it but it doesn't feel good, it's the Universe telling us that now is not the right time. This is especially true if there is something else calling your name.

It's important to know, too, that sometimes the things that your instincts are telling you to move toward or to do aren't necessarily "joyful" experiences. But sometimes your heart will tell you that you should be with a friend who is sick instead of going to a party where you are expected. If your gut is moving you towards something else, give yourself permission to do it.

#1 Rule for Receiving - No judgment

Sometimes we don't do what we want to do because we think people are watching and have opinions about us. That's bad. What's worse is that there is a 99% chance that what you think people are thinking isn't correct. Most people are so caught up in what they think *they* should be doing in other people's eyes that they aren't paying attention to what *you* are doing. Think about it. Why would the Universe move you toward something that you don't like or doesn't feel right? It just wouldn't! The Universe loves you and only wants you to do what you want to do. Get in alignment with what feels good and stop worrying about what other people think.

#2 Rule for Receiving - Surrender

Don't worry about when or how. You will manifest what you want. Relax and surrender to the Universe.

Abracadabra – bring me a car!

My husband Paul and I wanted to buy a car for our kids who were just getting their driver's licenses and needed a car to get back and forth to school. My husband, being a car aficionado, took to the task passionately. He researched the best-rated cars for safety and performance, he checked all the car sales websites, and dragged me to all of the used-car sales centers. I only had one rule: I wasn't spending more than $3,500 on this car. I didn't want to spend a lot, and I knew it was for local driving only. That was the dollar figure in my head, and I wasn't comfortable spending a penny more.

For weeks on end, my husband shopped and dragged me along for the ride. Car after car was well over my budget, and weekend after weekend I would hold my ground and remind him that these prices were beyond what I wanted to spend. He would argue that he wasn't finding any cars cute enough or safe enough for $3,500.

One very hot summer afternoon before we were due to be at a neighbor's party, my husband gave me an ultimatum. He showed me three cars on pages he had printed out and said, "you have to choose a car from these options; school is starting soon and the kids need a car, and there is nothing else for sale." The lowest priced one was $6,000. My reaction? "We are not spending more than $3,500 on a car for our kids, and I am not concerned that you haven't found a good one yet." Then I shouted my favorite affirmation:

EVERYTHING ALWAYS WORKS OUT FOR ME!

We put the conversation on hold and went across the street to the neighbor's party. When we arrived, the backyard was already crowded with people. I was very drawn to a patio table covered with a beautiful canopy that looked cool and comfortable. I sat down and noticed my favorite party food: spinach dip in a bowl carved out of pumpernickel bread! Yum! The only problem at this comfortable, shaded table was that the other people sitting there were the fathers and husbands of the families attending the party. The wives were all inside the house getting food ready, coming in and out to put out dishes and silverware. Each time one of the women came out to put out a salad fork or bring in some garbage they would say hello to me and head back in the kitchen.

I started to feel guilty. I thought, *I should be inside with the women and helping. I should be talking to them about what's going on in their lives and catching up on their kids' news. They probably think I'm being lazy and wondering why I am sitting out here with the men just eating spinach dip.*

But then I remembered that the Universe wants me to feel joy and wants me to stay where I feel my joy. It was wonderful sitting there, and I was grateful for the canopy, the comfortable chair, and my view of the beautiful yard. I felt the Universe telling me, "you feel good, stay put, stay out of the sun and eat the spinach dip. No need for small talk, just relax." I was so happy in this spot and thanked the Universe for giving it to me. I decided not to worry about what others might think of me. After I made the decision to stick with my joy and stay in my seat, I heard one of the men at the table say, "Hey, Bob, have you been able to sell your car yet?" I couldn't believe my ears. I perked up and said, "Bob, are you selling a car? That's such a coincidence because Paul and I have been debating about buying a car for the girls." Bob got visibly excited. He proceeded to tell me all about the features and benefits and upgrades he had put into this car. When he was done, I had to ask, "how much are you selling it for?" His answer was, "I will sell it to you for Blue Book value, $3,500." I knew this was the Law of Attraction at work; I couldn't help but give myself a high-five in my head for being so *powerful.*

I called Paul over to the table, who of course was pleased with the upgrades Bob described he had given his top-of-the-line car. And when he said that it was $3,500, my dear husband gave me that look that said *'Wow, you did it again! You are amazing!'* Within the next 45 minutes the title to the car was in our hands.

Your high vibes make the magic happen.

The Universe will deliver to us whatever we want. But it is our job to stay in a place of joy and not question how it will happen. If I had allowed myself to shift into a mindset of worrying about what other people think, if I had gotten up from the table because I felt like I *should* be helping in the kitchen, I would not have overheard that conversation. Instead of the struggle and all the work and the discomfort, all I needed to do was follow my gut and my heart and it led me right to where I could receive.

Staying in that place of joy keeps your vibration nice and high. It allows you to hear your heart and it reminds you of just how magical you and the Universe are. When you feel compelled to make a choice that's right for you, whether it's choosing an outfit, a rainy day activity, who to sit with in the cafeteria, or when to start a project, it's always going to bring you to the signs from the Universe. When you put out a vibration that's very high, you have power. You can hear the Universe talking to you.

CHAPTER 7

The Magic Words: Thank You

When you make peace with where you are, it automatically sets you in the direction of where you want to be.

— Abraham Hicks

Thank you. This all comes together at thank you. And I don't mean saying thank you when someone gives you something or offers you a beverage. I mean waking up in the morning and saying, "thank you!" to the Universe. Whenever you have a moment of happiness and laughter. Say thank you. Whenever you realize that your friends really do love you, say thank you. When you realize that you have a roof over your head, your health, a brother or sister to play with and fight with, say *thank you* to the Universe. When you feel down, remember just how much you have to be grateful for.

Find it even when it's hard.

What's most important is to say thank you even when something goes wrong. This is a tough one, but if something goes wrong and you feel bad, like the Universe is turning against you, you must find something in the moment to be grateful for and say thank you. If you're stuck in traffic and will miss an important client meeting, say thank you to the Universe for not being in the accident that caused the traffic. If you find out that you forgot to do an entire homework assignment the night before it's due, instead of being frustrated, say thank you to the Universe for reminding you so that you don't get a zero.

Why is this important? Because the more you can find the gratitude in every moment and appreciate what the Universe has given you, the more the Universe will give you to be thankful for! Not only that – and this is really important – if you're trying to manifest something, the magic of feeling your intuition and your gut pulling you in a certain direction only happens when you are in a high vibration. There are no higher vibrations than love and gratitude. If you're sad that something didn't go right in school, don't start thinking about everything else that's gone wrong with your day and worrying about how everything is going to just spiral out of control. Instead, find what there is to be grateful for as soon as possible. If something goes wrong in class, maybe someone made fun of you and the other kids laughed, notice who among the kids in your class supported you and be grateful for them. Be grateful for a good teacher that comes to your defense. Switch to gratitude as soon as possible at all times. Stay in as high a vibration as you can and keep your energy fun and light so that you can still know that the Universe is going to deliver what's perfect for you!

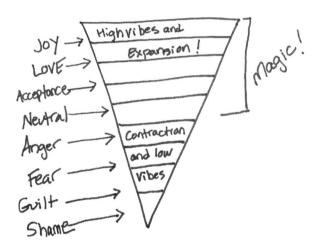

Take a look at this vibrational scale. This illustrates different emotions and how high or low the vibrational frequency of each is. The middle of the scale is neutral, and you can manifest things in those emotional states. But if you want to manifest faster, bring your emotions up higher on the scale, because this is where the Universe is going to be most responsive to you and it's where you're going to be able to "hear" and "see" the Universe pulling you in a certain direction. If you fall below the middle, you run the risk of your vibrational pull going further and further down. You will not feel your gut instincts anymore. Your sad emotional state will make you blind to the opportunities and components that are being presented to you.

Thank you – for rejecting me!

Peter was an eighth grader who was looking forward to graduating from middle school in a few months, but was even more excited about the possibility of attending a special exclusive high school that was focused on science. He knew that this program was for him not just because he liked the subject matter, but also because he liked the way the school program was structured and the small class sizes. It was perfect for him. Peter applied for the program and waited for the acceptance letters to come out.

The day arrived. Peter found the envelope in his mailbox with the science high school's return address on it. At first excited, everything went into slow motion for him when he saw among the first few words of the letter that he was not accepted to the program. He was distraught. Not only did he not get into the program, he was very disappointed that he would have to go to his regular town high school. Peter stayed in his room and cried for a few days. He kept imagining how crowded the local public high school was and how much homework there would be. He also was disappointed that he wouldn't have a chance to make new friends; yet another year going to school with the same kids he had been in school with for nine years already.

I spoke with Peter and told him that while everything seemed so hopeless, the worst thing he could do would be to let himself drop low on the vibrational scale. He had to find a way to climb back up to where he could start having happy days, where things manifest regularly and tend to work out instead of going wrong. So he started to think about all the good points of going to his public high school. For one thing, public school started a little later in the morning and it was only five minutes away; the science school was a 45-minute drive in each direction. Peter's older brother also encouraged him. He told Peter that there are many more extracurricular activities at the public school and that he would be there to show him the ropes and show him off. It made Peter smile to imagine already being on the inside track at high school with his big brother there to guide him. He began to really appreciate what he already had right in front of him, and when it came time to register for classes he saw all the opportunities in different subjects and enjoyed going through the vast catalog of courses at this large school.

It only took about 10 days for Peter to get himself back to a high vibration where he could appreciate what he already had, rather than focusing on the struggle of trying to get something else. He told me he realized that he had a lot to be grateful for. Just a few days after we spoke about his commitment to having an attitude of gratitude, he received a letter from the admissions director at the science high school. Peter could not believe his eyes when he read it—for the first time in many years, a spot opened up in the program after enrollment had begun, and he was invited to attend. Peter spent four amazing years at the science high school.

Thank you – for the lousy weather!

Tammy, a 16-year-old who had just started a part-time job working for a frozen yogurt eatery, was excited when the boss asked her to work a special all-day shift at a county fair. The money was going to be time and a half, and she was grateful because she really needed it to buy a car she wanted. Well, on the morning of the fair, the weather report was bad: humid and rainy. Tammy wasn't thrilled at the prospect of spending the day at an outdoor fair in the rain and heat. But since she was grateful for the opportunity, she decided that everything would work out and that the Universe would support her. As soon as she climbed up the vibrational scale from disappointment to gratitude, Tammy got a call from her boss who told her that since the fair wasn't likely to be too busy due to the weather, he didn't need her to work. But since Tammy had committed to going, her boss was going to pay her the regular rate for the day even though she didn't work.

Practice, practice, practice.

Gratitude is where the Universe meets you. This is where your vibration is at its highest form. When you are grateful for what you already have, the Universe delivers what you ask for. Never be afraid to appreciate what you have, even though ultimately you would really like something more. You can be in 100% alignment vibrationally with what you want to manifest while being in a state of thankfulness for your current situation.

Get into the practice of finding reasons to be grateful wherever you go. In the beginning of this book, your first project was to create a bookmark with 10 things on each side that you were grateful for. When you feel down and your vibration starts to drop, and you can't think of a way out of your low vibration on your own, just look at your bookmark! Look how much you have to be grateful for! And go do something that makes you feel joy or comfort. The sooner you can move out of your bad head space, the sooner you're back on track to get your magic working again so that you can manifest just what you want.

*** FAMILY TIME: Do this together at least weekly: Talk about what you're grateful for and discuss any challenges that came up for you during the week. Help each other find that spark of gratitude even in challenging times.

CHAPTER 8

More Stories of Magic!

How Trina Made Her Bullies Disappear

Remember Trina from the beginning of this book? Trina was in fourth grade and was having trouble with two girls at school who had been her best friends, Jenny and Leila. They had decided that they no longer wanted to include Trina in their little group, and not only did they not include her – they convinced the other girls in her class to not sit with her at lunch or talk to her. Of course, this made Trina very unhappy in school. But after learning about the Law of Attraction, she knew what to do.

Trina imagined what it would be like if Jenny and Leila weren't at school, as if they didn't even exist. She visualized getting off the bus, going into class, sitting with the girls that she used to have fun with before bullies told them to stay away from her, and she noticed how relaxed and liberated she felt. In addition to visualizing a new reality at school without her bullies present, Trina repeated one affirmation:

I have lots of friends at school,
everyone likes to be with me.

She repeated that affirmation as she fell asleep feeling wonderful. She imagined all the great friends around her, and that Jenny and Leila didn't even exist.

The next day Trina repeated her affirmation over and over in her mind until she arrived at school. She felt excited, as if the two bullies weren't at school.

Well, it turned out to be quite a day! Trina walked into class and noticed that Leila wasn't there. Perhaps she's sick, Trina thought. She sat down and one of the other girls in the class came over to say hello and show her the new cute gloves she got from her mom the night before. Trina felt great. She turned around and noticed Jenny behind her at her usual seat, but she appeared to shrink away when Trina turned to look at her. She felt very powerful! Then, just as class was starting, someone from the principal's office entered and called Jenny out of the classroom. Trina didn't see her for the rest of the day, but rumor had it that Jenny was being disciplined by the principal for bad behavior. At lunchtime, when approaching the table where the girls from her class sat in the cafeteria, Trina could not believe her ears when one of the girls called out her name and said, "Trina, come sit with me!" She sat down and other girls came over to sit with them, too. Trina described her time in the cafeteria as magical. It gave me great joy to hear her say, "About halfway through lunch I realized that I was doing all the talking, and that the other girls were listening to my stories and laughing with me."

I stayed in touch with Trina for several years after that. She was very active during middle school, she had lots of friends and worked on community service projects. Later, after attending the honors program at her high school, she got accepted to a wonderful college where she is sure to thrive. Trina learned when she was nine years old a great lesson about how powerful and magical she really is, and she will carry that with her for the rest of her life.

How Jennifer Went from Lonely to Super-Hot Mama

Jennifer was a single mom with two daughters, one in middle school and one in high school. She had made it through an awful marriage and an even worse divorce. Not surprisingly, Jennifer always worried about her kids and whether they would have healthy marriages as adults. This worry consumed her, and she frequently spoke to her daughters negatively about relationships.

But the worst thing about that bad marriage was that it led to Jennifer giving up on dating. She felt that there were no good men left in the world to have a relationship with. Even some nice guys at work were emotionally unavailable, and they never made eye contact with her. She told me that she lost hope of ever finding love again, and she decided that she was done with relationships. She admitted that she was sad about her decision, but accepted that this was how it would be for the rest of her life, and it somehow took the pressure off of her to find love.

I spoke with Jennifer and convinced her that the dating scene she disliked so much was the result of her thoughts, and that she had the power to change the whole situation. I taught her about her vibration and that the energy that was emanating from her was her decision to be single for the rest of her life. How could she possibly attract others into her life when she asked the Universe to keep her single like that?

When I asked her about what kind of relationship she wanted, Jennifer immediately thought of an older couple she had seen in the parking lot at the grocery store the day before. The woman was using a scooter due to a handicap, and her husband was walking at a slow pace next to her with his hand gently placed on her back. It made Jennifer long for that kind of unconditional love and companionship. Now that she had that feeling behind what she felt was true love, I was able to guide her to visualize what it would be like to love a man deeply and unconditionally like that and have it reflected back to her equally. I also gave her two affirmations to say as she fell asleep that night with that wonderful warm feeling, as if it was already real:

"I am in an exciting and wonderful relationship."
"There are so many great men around me all the time!"

I told Jennifer that on her way to work she should feel really excited to know that her next boyfriend was just around the corner. She should feel so excited about it that she wouldn't be able to stop smiling. She promised to do what I said, and three days later I received a text from her: "I cannot believe how my last three days have gone! First, when I got to work the morning after my visualization and affirmations, one of my really cute coworkers that never looked up at me before, suddenly did. We struck up the first conversation we've ever had. He even asked where I go grocery shopping and said we should meet there some time. He, too, was divorced, and I think something is building there!" I was so excited for her! We met four weeks later for lunch and she looked absolutely stunning. "You would not believe how my month has been," Jennifer said. "I am seeing two different men right now, and they are lots of fun. I don't know if they are marriage material or not, but I am having the best time!"

Yikes! Your Magic Power Works Even when you aren't trying!

Early in my career I worked for a nonprofit organization. It was a good job with many perks, one of which was attending an international conference of other nonprofits throughout the world. One summer, the conference was in Atlanta, a huge vibrant city known for its great food and entertainment. I was with a coworker, Eva, who loved to travel and was even more excited than I was. When we arrived, Atlanta was pulsating with energy as more than 15,000 people had descended on the city to attend this event. The conference logo was everywhere—the airport, on taxis, written in neon lights at the top of several skyscrapers; this conference was HUGE! The conference programming was great and we were learning a lot. The only problem was that whenever there was a break, Eva would mutter under her breath about a past coworker she knew at her previous job, also at a nonprofit. "I really hope I don't run into Joanna here. She's a horrible person and I couldn't wait to get away from her when I left that organization."

Everywhere we went, for some reason Eva was triggered by memories of Joanna. I warned her to let it go and wipe Joanna from her mind because not only would she be happier if she forgot about it, she was very close to unleashing the Law of Attraction and running head-on into her arch nemesis. But no matter what we were doing, Eva would make a remark about Joanna.

On the last night of the conference, Eva and I hit the town to find a place with good music and good drinks. While on a city shuttle bus, we noticed a cool jazz club and agreed to jump off the shuttle to check it out. When we got inside and were seated, we both remarked how welcoming the club felt. A woman with an intoxicating voice was singing popular R&B songs on a stage in the back of the club when our Cosmo martinis arrived, and we relaxed and started to discuss all we had learned throughout the week. Eventually the singer finished out her set and welcomed everyone to the club. After introducing her accompanist, she said, "I have a special message for someone right now. Joanna Smith, your friends wanted me to wish you a happy birthday. Why don't you come on up here and we'll all sing Happy Birthday to you?" Eva's face went white.

There, up on the stage at this club, one of hundreds of clubs in Atlanta, a city currently 15,000 people over its usual population, was the very person Eva least wanted to see. I smiled and winked at her.

"Lesson learned," she admitted.

CHAPTER 9

Bonus Experiment

Certain words and symbols have a high vibration that creates positive outcomes on the world. Likewise, when words that are negative are directed at others, they can have a horrible impact on people and the environment around us.

Dr. Masaru Emoto, an expert in the field of energy and vibration, has illustrated that human consciousness has an effect on the molecular structure of water. In his most famous of studies, he subjected water to various words and conditions, then he flash-froze the water and studied the patterns of the molecules. Classical music, loving words, and exposure to individuals who make a positive impact on the world resulted in structures that, under a microscope, took on beautiful and ornate shapes. Conversely, water exposed to words of hate and neglect and images of people who created destruction in our history, morphed these water molecules into shapes with no pattern and appeared beaten and weary.

For your interest, I highly recommend looking up Dr. Emoto and his experiments with water molecules and watching some related videos. You will certainly be impacted by observing the difference a few words and negative vibrations can make.

Dr. Emoto also created the following rice and water experiment. It is another testament to our power to affect life around us with our vibration. The best part: it's easy to try at home!

Instructions

1. Place equal amounts of rice and water in two jars.
2. Using paper and tape, mark one jar "Love" and the other "Hate."
3. Place the jars in the same environment, like on your kitchen counter or on a windowsill with the same amount of light, but at least 12 inches apart.
4. Every day speak to each jar, but treat them differently. Tell the jar marked "Love" that you love it and say thank you to it. Treat the jar marked "Hate" badly. Tell it you don't like it and call it names, like "idiot."

After a week or so, you will be shocked to see how the jar that's been shown love and gratitude thrives much better than the jar that received negative energy. Within a month you will see mold growing at a more rapid pace on the jar marked "Hate."

Think about this experiment and Dr. Emoto when you start to lose your temper or have negative thoughts about the people and situations in your life. Your energy and vibration are powerful—choose to use your power for good!

CHAPTER 10

Special Project – Make a Vision Board!

Visualizing, with the emotion that comes with imagining that you have already manifested what you want, is your most powerful tool for getting in alignment with the right vibration to attract the results that you want. A vision board is a great tool to supplement this practice.

This is a good project for families, roommates, or your group of friends to do together. After you have gone through this book and fully understand what it means to ask, believe, and receive, you are ready to build a vision board to help you manifest!

Materials

- Poster board
- Glue
- Magazines and other image sources

Instructions

1. Take a look at the list of things that you want to manifest. Find images in magazines or by doing an Internet search that represent what you want. The images don't have to be an exact match; all that is required is that when you look at that image, you know in your mind what it means to you. Words and symbols work as well.

2. Arrange the images on your poster board and glue them down.

3. Find a place in your home or office to place your vision board. It should be a place that you are around a lot where you have time to lock your eyes and feelings on it. This could be in your bedroom if that's where you want to spend some focused time every day, or it could be on your bulletin board in your office, or where you do your homework, etc.

4. Whenever you can, spend a few moments in meditation. Close your eyes, take some deep breaths, and try to empty your mind for five

minutes. Set an alarm so you can totally relax. When you open your eyes look at your vision board. Focus on each item for several moments as you imagine how it will feel to manifest each one. Remember to make it feel as real as possible, like it has already manifested for you. Close out your session by saying affirmations tied to each thing on your vision board.

Great news! Even when you don't have time to go through the process, just having the vision board where you can see it often will start to rewire your brain so that you can use your magic powers to manifest what you want. *You are always connected to the Universe with the Law of Attraction!*

Go use your magic!

Now that you know how to use your magic power, the power of the Law of Attraction, you'll begin to experience synchronicities and coincidences all the time. You'll think of someone fondly and they'll appear in front of you within hours. You'll try to remember the name of your favorite movie from when you were a kid and the DJ will mention it on the radio, you'll wish you had the phone number of a fellow school parent you met years earlier and you'll bump into them in the grocery store.

If you saw the movie *The Karate Kid*, you won't forget the lesson learned by the young main character Daniel (or Dre if you saw the remake): by practicing the same motions and mindset over and over, you internalize them so deeply that it is effortless to implement when needed.

> The best way to practice using your
> magic is to wake up each day
> remembering your power,
> deciding what you want, and
> feeling grateful.

Take a deep breath, exhale, and smile. You have the power of the Universe within you. Now go create the life that you want!

ABOUT THE AUTHOR

While she wasn't always aware that there was a name for what she was doing, Mary Petto has been leveraging the Law of Attraction since she was a teenager. Many years after she manifested her very first boyfriend, she was introduced to the Law of Vibration at a professional development program sponsored by her employer. It was then that she began her practice of the "fake it till you make it" theory, a popular way to move ahead in one's career that few understand is based on the Law of Vibration—and it certainly worked for her. Mary became a young executive in the financial services world just as she had always dreamed. Her marketing career took off, and eventually she manifested a consulting business, creating marketing plans and social media strategies during the early years of Facebook and Twitter for entrepreneurs, authors, doctors, environmental experts, and magazines.

It was many years later that Mary discovered the book *The Secret. The Secret* was eye-opening for her because it helped her understand that she had been practicing the Law of Attraction techniques without even realizing it. She got back into proactively harnessing the magic for herself, and dedicated years to helping adults and children manifest the lives they wanted, spreading awareness of the Law of Attraction and creating personalized practices for tapping into the Universal Source.

In addition to private Law of Attraction coaching, Mary speaks to audiences of all sizes and is a regular contributor to *Thrive Global* and other publications.

Printed in the United States
By Bookmasters